Contents

Words in **bold** are in the glossary on page 28.

All about me

My name is Fahad Ismail and I am 10 years old. My family are **refugees** from Somalia. I speak **Somali** and English.

Football is my favourite hobby. I play all the time!

Meeting people

Try talking in Somali!

Hello
Salaam aleikum

How are you?
Scowarran ('scow' as in 'cow')

I'm fine, thank you
Wan fi anna hi

(Look out for more Somali words in this book.)

I love sport. My favourite game is football and I play as a striker for my local team, the Somali Ranger Boys. I also enjoy cricket and rounders – I can run really fast!

Moving to Britain from
Somalia

By Cath Senker
Photography by Howard Davies

FRANKLIN WATTS
LONDON•SYDNEY

First published in 2008 by Franklin Watts

Franklin Watts,
338 Euston Road,
London, NW1 3BH

Franklin Watts Australia,
Level 17/207 Kent Street,
Sydney, NSW 2000

Series editor: Sarah Peutrill
Art director: Jonathan Hair
Design: Rita Storey
Photographs: Howard Davies (unless otherwise stated)

The Author and Photographer would like to thank the following for their help in the preparation of this book: The Gulzar-e-Habib Mosque, Darnall; Ifrah Harun; Ruweida Hussein; Mohamed, Fahad and Hamse Ismail; Mohamed Mah, Fahad's football coach; Ian Martin, Northern Refugee Centre (NRC); Yasmin Mohamud from NRC and Link Action Community Organisation; the staff and pupils of Phillimore Community School, Darnall, Sheffield, especially Sara Griffiths, Class 12 (2006–07) and Angela Wild; Asiya Qasse.

Picture credits: Kevin Fleming/Corbis: 13.
Every attempt has been made to clear copyright. Should there be any inadvertent omission please apply to the publisher for rectification.

Dewey number: 304.8'41'06773

ISBN: 978 0 7496 7862 3

Printed in China

Franklin Watts is a division of Hachette Children's Books, an Hachette Livre UK company.

link community
action organisation

northern refugee centre

I like riding my bike, playing on
my Playstation and reading.

Our street is
not too busy so
I can cycle
safely.

I like Somali food as well as English meals
such as pizza and burgers. Mum makes
lovely rice and meat, and great chips too.

Mum is making
salad to go with
lunch. We often
eat rice cooked
with raisins and
spices. On top
we have meat
sauce.

Meet my family

I live with my mum and two brothers in Sheffield in the north of England. My older brother Mohamed is 13 and my younger brother Hamse is 9.

Family words

Mother	*Hooyo*
Father	*Abba*
Brother/Sister	*Walaal*

My mum's sister Ifrah lives in London but I don't have any other family in the UK.

Here I am with my younger brother Hamse. Aunt Ifrah has come to visit and is serving our lunch.

Here I'm playing a great game called kerbie with my older brother Mohamed. You have to throw the ball to hit the kerb to win points.

Mum is a volunteer with the Somali **Peer** Support Project. Some Somali children have problems at school, especially boys. Mum helps the parents to cope with the problems so their children can get a good education.

Mum and Aunt Yasmin are discussing plans for their project. (We Somalis call close adult friends 'Aunt' or 'Uncle'.)

About Somalia

Somalia is in eastern Africa. Many people are **nomads**. They rely on their sheep, cattle and goats to make a living. Others are farmers, growing bananas, **sorghum**, corn, coconuts and rice.

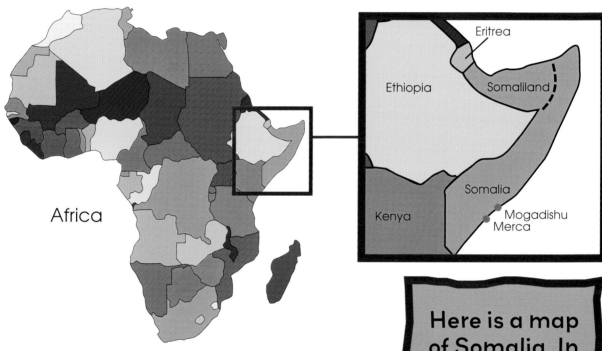

Africa

Eritrea

Ethiopia

Somaliland

Somalia

Kenya

Mogadishu
Merca

Since 1991, Somalia has had no strong **government**. A **civil war** rages between rival groups. In 2006, an **Islamic** organisation took over a large part of the country.

Here is a map of Somalia. In the north, Somaliland calls itself a separate country from Somalia.

The government's forces fought back, with help from Ethiopia and the USA.

There are many groups of young men fighting the government in Somalia.

The civil war has ruined the country. Most people live in **poverty**. Many schools and hospitals have been destroyed.

Aunt Yasmin says:

"The main problem in Somalia today is the civil war. None of the country's problems can be solved until there is peace."

Large numbers of Somalis do not have a clean water supply. Here, the charity Oxfam has provided a water tap.

My life in Somalia

I come from a village called Golweyn, near Merca in southern Somalia. Golweyn is about two hours by road from the capital, Mogadishu.

At school I used the white board to show my class where Somalia is on the map.

Most people in the village make their living from farming.

Our home in Somalia had a courtyard in the middle. We had a big garden with trees to give shade. I can just about remember our house and playing with my uncle in the garden.

Numbers from 1 to 10

One	Kow
Two	Labba
Three	Saddex
Four	Afar
Five	Shan
Six	Lix
Seven	Todoba
Eight	Sideed
Nine	Sajaal
Ten	Toban

Moving to Britain

Life was terrible in Somalia because of the civil war. Sometimes there was fighting in our village, and homes were hit by **mortars**. My dad was killed in the war. Mum did not feel safe looking after three young boys on her own.

Mum brought the three of us to Britain to be safe.

This is a view of Sheffield towards the city centre. When we first arrived, we were amazed by the size of the buildings.

We flew to London in the UK when I was four. It took two days to reach London. When we arrived, we went to the **Home Office** to claim **asylum**. They gave us somewhere to stay in London for four months. Then we were sent to live in Sheffield in South Yorkshire.

Fahad's mum says:

"It was so hard at first because we didn't speak English. Hamse was in a car accident and I didn't even know where to take him."

My new hometown

We've had to move eight times since we came to Sheffield. Now we live in an area called Darnall.

There used to be lots of factories in Sheffield. Opposite our house, there was once a steelworks. Steel, cutlery and machinery are still made in Sheffield. The city has lots of big shops and fun things to do.

In Somalia, most people depend on their **livestock** or crops for food. Here, you can buy everything in the shops.

I like it here because I'm able to go to school. I have friends from several countries. There are plenty of places to go, such as the swimming pool and the library. We didn't have these things in Somalia.

Fahad's mum says:

"When we first arrived, it was hard to get around. We had to get two buses to get to school and it was very confusing."

We often go to our local library. Here I'm looking at a map of the UK in an atlas.

Going to school

I started school in Reception soon after we arrived in the UK. I only spoke a little English. A language support teacher used to help me until I could speak English well.

Mum usually takes us to school. Sometimes Aunt Yasmin picks us up – the mums help each other.

School words

School	*School* (same word)
Teacher	*Macalin* (say 'maalin')
Student	*Arday*
Class	*Class* (same word)
Table	*Miis*
Book	*Buuo*
Pencil	*Khalin qori*

Now I'm in Year 5 at Phillimore Community School. It takes about 15 minutes to walk there. It's a really good school.

My best friend at school is Isaac. His family is from Pakistan.

There are many kids from English, Pakistani, Bangladeshi and Somali families. Recently, some Polish and Czech children have joined the school. We all work well together.

Here I am at playtime running around with my friends. I always like to keep active.

My school day

My teacher is Miss Griffiths. I love Maths and PE. I'm in the top group in Maths and I'm fantastic at PE! I'm also keen on Science, especially when we do experiments.

In our Science lesson today, we are learning about the water cycle. Miss Griffiths is telling us about evaporation and how clouds form.

I like reading but I'm not so keen on writing. It's hard to remember punctuation rules and spellings.

Here we are on the carpet for the literacy lesson, comparing the film of *The Lion, the Witch and the Wardrobe* to the book.

At lunchtime I have school dinner. I like the healthy menu. Afterwards I play football for the rest of break.

Miss Griffiths says:

"Fahad is a really keen student and I enjoy teaching him. He is a clever and thoughtful boy who always asks interesting questions."

Free time

In Somalia, when there was no fighting, we were free to play outdoors. The roads were not as dangerous as in the UK. We made our own toys or played games such as hide and seek.

At home we often play simple games. Hamse and our friend Ruweida like playing noughts and crosses.

In the UK, our activities are more organised. On Saturdays I go to a homework club at the Pakistani **Muslim** Centre in Darnall. As well as doing schoolwork, there are different activities. Sometimes we go on trips, for example to Chester Zoo.

I'm very keen on football and take the training seriously.

Every Sunday afternoon I go to football training in my local park.

Mohamed, Fahad's football coach says:

"Fahad is a talented player. He's very fit, a fast runner and an excellent striker – and he understands how to work well in a team."

Keeping our culture

I like mixing with all different people, but at home we keep up our Somali **traditions**.

Sometimes for breakfast we eat **anjera**, which is like a pancake. It's very tasty with sesame oil or with butter and jam. My favourite Somali meal is pasta with tomato and meat sauce.

Usually we have cornflakes for breakfast, but today Mum has made anjera as a treat.

Like most Somalis, my family is Muslim. Every day after school I go to classes at the **mosque** to learn to read the **Qur'an**. My brother Mohamed has already learnt the whole Qur'an.

I can read **Arabic** as easily as English and I've learnt many parts of the Qur'an by heart.

Aunt Yasmin says:

"We celebrate the festival of **Id-ul-Fitr** with other Muslims. After prayers at the mosque, we put on new clothes. We enjoy a festive meal of lamb and rice with raisins and spices."

At Id-ul-Fitr and other festivals, we burn incense in a dabqad – it means 'fire holder'. It is a Somali tradition.

My future

I like living in Sheffield and hope our family is allowed to stay in the UK. Mum is planning to train as a nurse so she can earn a living in this country. When I grow up, I would like to go to **university** and train for a professional job, perhaps as a doctor or a bank manager.

I want to do well at school so I'll have plenty of job **opportunities** when I'm older.

My greatest ambition though is to be a professional footballer. Maybe I'll be the first Somali refugee to play for England!

Here I am, about to score a goal!

Fahad's mum says:

"All my sons have plans for the future. Mohamed wants to be a doctor, Fahad a footballer and Hamse a singer and dancer. I would like them to be able to achieve their dreams."

Glossary

anjera
A Somali pancake made from sorghum and teff, a grain from a type of grass that grows in northern Africa.

Arabic
The main language of several countries in North Africa and the Middle East. It is also the language of Islam.

asylum
Protection given to people who have left their country because they were in danger. Refugees have to claim asylum when they reach Britain.

civil war
A war between groups of people in the same country.

government
A group of people who have the power to make and enforce laws for a country.

Home Office
A government department in the UK that is in charge of the law inside the country. The Home Office decides if refugees can stay in the UK.

Id-ul-Fitr
A Muslim festival that comes at the end of the Muslim month of Ramadan.

Islamic
Something or someone that belongs to the religion of Islam.

livestock
The animals people keep for their meat, milk and skins, such as sheep and goats.

mortars
Bombs fired by a heavy gun.

mosque
A place of worship for followers of Islam.

Muslim
A member of the religion of Islam.

nomads
Nomads are people who move from place to place with their animals, looking for good grazing land.

opportunities
Chances to do something.

peer
Someone who is around the same age as you and in a similar situation.

poverty
When someone has little or no money or few possessions.

Qur'an
The holy book of Islam.

refugees
Refugees are people who have been forced to leave their own country because it is too dangerous to stay there.

Somali
The main language spoken in Somalia.

sorghum
A grass that can be grown in hot, dry countries. It is an important food crop in Africa.

traditions
Things that people have done or believed in for a long time.

university
A place where some people go to study when they have left school.

Somalia fact file

Location:
Eastern Africa, with Ethiopia to the west and the Indian Ocean to the east

Climate:
Mostly desert

Capital city:
Mogadishu

Population:
About nine million

Life expectancy at birth (the average age people live to):
49

Main religion:
Islam

Language:
Somali. Arabic, Italian and English are also spoken

Literacy (the percentage of people over 15 who can read and write):
38%

Main jobs:
71% make their living from farming

Number of Somali refugees:
460,000. Around 400,000 Somalis are internally displaced (they have had to leave their homes but are still in Somalia)

Index

Further information

BBC News Country Profile: Somalia
http://news.bbc.co.uk/1/hi/world/africa/country_profiles/1072592.stm

CIA World Factbook
https://www.cia.gov/library/publications/the-world-factbook/geos/so.html

Note to parents and teachers: Please note that these websites are **not** specifically for children and we strongly advise that Internet access is supervised by a responsible adult.